CROCHET PATTERNS FOR CHRISTMAS ORNAMENTS

Gorgeous Easy-To-Make Crochet Ornaments To Prepare Your Home For The Christmas Miracle

By

SAMANTHA WHITE

Contents

Crochet Patterns for Christmas Ornaments:

Gorgeous Easy-To-Make Crochet Ornaments To Prepare Your Home For The Christmas Miracle

Do you recall how excited you get every year when you pull out your Christmas ornaments and recall what you like about each one? Christmas ornaments can be a huge part of the homey, comfortable Christmas memories we develop with our family and friends every year.

Making your own Christmas ornaments is a great experience.

However, you are not required to keep all of your ornaments to yourself! Because the crocheted Christmas ornament patterns in this book bare simple to make, they are ideal for selling or gifting to friends.

Make some for your local Christmas craft market, distribute them at work, or consider include them as a finishing touch to your purchased gifts.

Introduction

Christmas is almost here, and it's a joyous time of year. Take in the beautiful lights and embellished trees all around you. The next time you visit someone's residence Take note of all the glitzy decorations that would warm your heart. Crochet Christmas wreaths are a great project to work on right before the holidays.

In honor of the holiday Hang it on your front door to greet visitors and family. Also make great gifts, but who doesn't like free crochet pattern. A free crochet wreath pattern isn't just for hanging on the door. It can also be turned into a tree ornament.

Christmas crochet patterns, specifically Christmas wreaths. Despite the fact that while there are only a few patterns in the book, you will enjoy what you see, so get started.

Don't be intimidated if this is your first holiday season making crochet Christmas patterns!

This collection includes simple Christmas crochet patterns for beginners as well as more intricate designs for intermediate-advanced crocheters. While you're at it, you might even discover a new crochet technique.

The favorite aspect about crocheting hand - made decorations is that you can tailor them to your personal tastes. This list includes minimalist crochet patterns that can be worn all winter as well as Christmas Season colors like pine-tree-green and Santa-suit-red. Whatever style you prefer these various patterns are a great way to bring the holiday spirit into your home.

CHAPTER 1

Crochet Supplies

You've probably noticed how quickly time passes in December, right? When planning to crochet Christmas patterns, make sure you have all of the necessary supplies on hand. This will assist you in having the most relaxing Xmas crochet season possible.

In addition to yarn, here are some materials you should keep on hand.

• A crochet hook (in size needed to obtain pattern gauge, if relevant)

• Tapestry needle - for weaving in ends and eventually joining pieces together

• A blocking board is particularly useful for lacy snowflakes and granny squares.

• A steamer or iron with a steam feature - for stifling specific projects (alternative: use a spray bottle)

Optional supplies to consider provide a project bag to hold your WIP (work in progress), scissors, a pom pom maker, buttons, leather accents, and, of course, the movie Love Actually.

Abbreviations

Dc   double crochet

ch(s)   chain(s)

ch-sp   chain space

dtr stands for double treble crochet (yo hook 3 times)

rep hdc   half double crochet

rnd   round

sc   single crochet

or sl st(s)	slip stitch(es)
sp(s)	space(s)
st(s)	stitch(es)
tr	treble crochet
yo	yarn over

Repeat the instructions the specified number of times after the symbol or enclosed by two symbols.

[Repeat the instructions enclosed within the brackets the number of times specified].

CHAPTER 2

Considerations When Using Crochet

Because Christmas is always on December 25th, you get a set deadline to complete your crochet works. If you're crocheting gifts, you should think about how long a pattern will take and the amount of time you have available.

In general, a simple pattern will:

• have fewer color changes (and therefore ends to weave in)

• Will be a smaller overall size

• Will not require much seaming

If you have the time, don't be afraid to take on a larger project. Snuggling under a C2C crochet Christmas blanket or hanging a set of handmade stockings could be the most enjoyable tradition.

Crochet Yarn for Christmas

If you want to make a Christmas tree dress or a mini Christmas tree, you may be wondering how to select the best yarn for your project.

Begin by inspecting the yarn specified in the pattern. Is a specific fiber, such as cotton, required? Or perhaps a specific yarn thickness, such as worsted weight or super bulky? Perhaps it makes no difference, and the pattern could be made with just about any yarn (like a snowflake or stuffed animal).

Think about washability.

If you're giving the item as a gift, choose an easy-care yarn. Find a machine-washable acrylic or wool blend, for example. This way, the recipient will not feel overburdened by caring for your handmade gift.

When purchasing yarn, consider whether you'll be able to reuse it for other Christmas crochet works. A single skein of white woollen weight yarn, for example, could be used to crochet numerous gnome beards, a few snowflakes, and a crochet snowman.

CHAPTER 3

Ornamental Patterns

Snowflakes patterns

Traditional Christmas crochet includes snowflakes. For a quick snowflake, use embroidery thread or worsted weight yarn. These free crochet snowflake patterns are suitable for decorating Christmas gifts, make a winter garland, and more. I love crocheted snowflakes. Their almost endless design options make them fascinating to crochet, and their lacy beauty makes them excellent as Christmas tree decorations, package ties, or lightcatchers.

Despite the complex shapes, snowflakes are easy and quick to create. All may be crocheted in an hour or less, and none require more than four rounds.

All may be crocheted in an hour or less, and none require more than four rounds. Instructions abbreviations are below.

Snowflakes were crocheted with DMC Cebelia1 cotton thread. I utilized sizes 10, 20, and 30 to get as many sizes as possible. I made the snowflake with the hook size specified in the instructions. Since everyone crochets differently, you may require a larger or smaller hook. You can make your snowflake bigger or smaller. Changing the thread and hook sizes does the trick. Remember to crochet the snowflake securely.

I added Balger's Metallic Blending Filament, White #100.2 to the snowflakes for shine. This tiny filament adds sparkle without changing the size of the snowflake. Hold the blending filament and crochet thread together and work with them as a single thread.

After crocheting, block and starch your snowflake. Wash it in warm water with mild soap if it's dirty. Rinse and dry with a towel.

Snowflakes can be stiffened in numerous ways. Spray or liquid starch won't give the piece adequate substance, so don't use it. Sugar starch is a good, albeit messy, commercial starch replacement. Small pan of sugar and water. Let the mixture cool to room temperature after boiling. Dilute white craft glue with water. I've never used commercial lace stiffeners.

Trace the blocking guide3 onto tissue or tracing paper and stretch the arms to the desired size. Place the guide on a pinning board, such as foam, fabric, or cardboard.

BEGINNING

Wrap or wax the guide. Immerse the snowflake in stiffening solution. Soak the snowflake for a few minutes, then carefully press out the excess solution. Right-side-up, pin the snowflake over the blocking guide. Begin at the middle and align the snowflake's points with the blocking guide's arms.

Pin each picot just after points. Before withdrawing the pins, let the snowflake dry.

To hang a snowflake, tie a loop using white or translucent thread.

SNOWFLAKE 1

Around 3" in diameter

Materials

10 yards DMC Cebelia #20

Steel crochet hook size 10

Ch 8 and sl st together to form a ring.

Rnd 1: Ch 3 (counts as a dc), 23 dc in ring, join in top of ch 3.

Rnd 2: [Ch 5, dtr in same sp, skip 2 dc, dtr in next dc, ch 5, sl st in same dc, ch 5, sl st in next dc, ch 5]

6 times [sl st in next dc] Rnd 3: Turn, slip stitch to the top of the ch-6 loop, turn, ch 5, dtr

Ch 3, sl st in 3rd ch from hook for picot, sl st in last dtr created, dtr in same sp

ch 6, sl st in the same loop, [ch 5, sl st in 4th ch above hook for picot]

[sl st in next ch and in bottom of next picot, ch 4, sl st in 4th ch from hook, 3 times]

Rep from 5 times with sl st in same picot, sl st in next ch and in ch-6 loop.

Close the loop.

SNOWFLAKE 2

Approximately 2.14 inches in diameter

Materials

6 yards DMC Cebelia #20

Steel crochet hook size 10

Ch 8 and sl st together to form a ring.

Rnd 1: Ch 7 (counts as dtr and ch 2), dtr in ring, ch 5, [dtr, ch 2, dtr in ring, ch 5], repeat from * to *.

5] Repeat 5 times; connect in the 5th ch of ch 7. Rnd 2: Work 2 sl sts in the next ch-2 sp, sl st in the next ch-2 sp, sl st in the next ch-2 sp

next dtr and 3 sc and 1 dc in same ch-5 sp, ch 6, dc in last dc

formed, ch 6, sl st in same dc, ch 1, 3 sc in same ch-5

sp, sl st in next dtr; repeat 5 times, finishing last repeat with a sl st in the initial sl st of the row.

rnd. Close the loop.

SNOWFLAKE 3

The diameter is approximately 2.12".

Materials

6 yards DMC Cebelia #20

Steel crochet hook size 10

Ch 8 and sl st together to form a ring.

Rnd 1: Ch 3 (counts as dc), 2 dc in ring, ch 2, [3 dc in ring, ch 2] 5 times; join in the first round.

top of chapter 3

Rnd 2: Ch 6 (counts as tr and ch 2), dc in first 3-dc group center dc, ch 2, tr in

dtr in next ch-2 sp, ch 3, [tr in first dc of next 3-dc group, ch 2, dc] 5 times [dc in next dc, ch 3, tr in next dc, ch 3, dtr in next ch-2 sp, ch 3]; connect in 4th

6th chapter

Rnd 3: Ch 1, *[3 sc in next ch-sp] 3 times, sc in dtr, ch 4, sc in same st, 3 sc in next ch-sp] 3 times, sc in dtr, ch 4, sc in same st, 3

next ch-sp; 5 reps from *; join in first sc Close the loop.

SNOWFLAKE 4

Around 3" in diameter

Materials

6 yards DMC Cebelia #10.

Steel crochet hook size 7

Ch 8 and sl st together to form a ring.

Rnd 1: Ch 1, [sc, dc, sc in ring] 6 times more; join in first sc.

Rnd 2: Ch 1, sc in same sp, *work hdc, dc, and hdc in next dc, sc in next 2 sc; repeat from * to *.

Rep from * 5 times more, finishing with a sl st in the first sc on the last repeat.

Rnd 3: Ch 1, sc in same sp, *ch 8, dtr in next dc, ch 4, sl st in 4th ch from hook, repeat from * to end.

sl st in newly created dtr, ch 8, sc between next 2 sc, [ch 6, sl st in 6th ch from hook]

for picot] twice, sl st in first ch-6 picot base, sc between same two sc; rep

Repeat from * 5 times, finishing with a sl st in the first sc on the last repeat. Close the loop.

SNOWFLAKE 5

Approximately a 234-inch diameter

Materials

10 yards DMC Cebelia #10.

Steel crochet hook size 7

Ch 8 and sl st together to form a ring.

Rnd 1: Ch 3 (counts as dc), 3 dc in ring, ch 1, [4 dc in ring, ch 1] 5 times; join in the first round.

top of chapter 3Rnd 2: Ch 3, dc in same sp, dc in each of the next 2 dc, 2 dc in next dc, ch 1, [2 dc in next dc]

in the next dc, dc in each of the following two dc, 2 dc in the next dc, ch 1] 5 times; connect in the top of the ch3.

Rnd 3: Ch 1, sc in same sp, *sc in next 5 dc, **ch 4, 2 dc in 4th ch from hook, repeat from * to *.

ch 3, sl st in same ch**, sc in next ch-1 sp on ring, ch 7, 2 tr in 5th ch from hook, ch 7, 2 tr in 5th ch from hook, ch 7, 2 tr in 5th ch from hook,

Rep between ch 4, sl st in same ch, sl st in next 2 ch, sc in same ch-1 sp on ring

**s once, sc in same ch-1 sp on ring, sc in next dc; rep from * 5 times, finishing with a sc in next dc

Finish with a sl st in the first sc. Close the loop.

CHAPTER 4

Crocheted Candy Cane Wreath

This crochet wreath is stunning decorated with candy canes and seems ideal for the holiday season season.

Materials:

•White and red 4 ply yarn

•1 pound Chenille stems

•12-inch Styrofoam wreath

•florist U shape pins (available in the flower section of the majority of craft stores Typically, Styrofoam is used.wreaths)

•Crochet hook or hook size H required to achieve gauge

Gauge:

4 hdc stitches = 1 inch, 3 rows hdc = 1 inch

CANE CANDY 6

Carry dropped yarn under stitches as you work.

Steps:

Ch-4 with White and H hook, sl st to

Make a ring.

RND 1: Ch-1, 2 hdc in the ring, join

Drop Red, 1 hdc in ring, drop

Start picking up Red, drop White, 2 hdc in ring

Start picking up White, 1 hdc in ring drop Red, grab White, 2 hdc in

Need not turn the ring.

RESIDUAL RNDS: (Drop White, select) red up, hdc next st, red down, red up

White, hdc next 2 sts) all the way around until the item measures 5-12"

Insert a previously cut chenille stem. folded in half and gently bent to Keep tog. Red, fasten off, and take up

White, hdc dec the next 2 stitches till

Fasten off once the aperture is closed.

Form into a candy cane shape.

-create 13 candy canes

Make 5 sweets by reversing the color. canes.

WRAP WITH OCHET RIBBON

ROW 1: Ch-8 with White and H hook,

hdc third chain from hook, hdc next two chains, Join Red, drop White, and hdc the last three chains. Turn with ch=1. (6 sts)

ROW 2: Hdc the next 3 stitches, drop Red, pick up

hdc last 3 stitches, ch-1, turn

ROW 3: Hdc the next 3 stitches, drop White,

Pick up Red, hdc last three stitches, ch-1, turn.

Rows 2-3 should be repeated until the piece measures

Fasten off at 137" long.

Pin the flowers with the U-shaped florist pins.

One end of the ribbon to the wreath, delicately wrap the wreath in taking care not to overlap the ribbon

Fasten the edges with another U pin.

Arrange the candy canes with care. onto the wreath, which holds them in place

Put the U pins in place.

Crochet Wreath with Christmas Bells

Lily Sugar'n Cream's

Crochet beautiful white Christmas bells

Add holly leaves for a festive look this holiday season, a wreath Crochet is a pleasurable pastime and low-cost approach to adorn.

BASIC VINE WREATHS 7

Materials:

•Lily Sugar'n Cream Yarn

2.5 oz [70.9 g] Cotton 4 ply Solids

g]; 2 oz. Sparkles [56.7 g] 1 ball

35 holly leaves are created. 1 pound of

Sparkle produces 15 bells.

1 ball of color A (Dk Pine)

1 ball in color B (White Tinsel)

•4 mm (U.S.) crochet hook

crochet hook (G or 6) or size required to
obtain a gauge

•14 in [10 mm] gold beads diameter with
a brass coating

12 yard [.5 meter] wire for Bells

•112 yards [1.4 meters] white ribbon

1 inch [2.5 cm] with gold trim wide enough for a large bow

•1 yard [.9 meter] red ribbon K in For little bows, [12 mm] broad

•8 dried tiny pine cones

•Glue gun, as well as glue sticks

•13-inch grape vine wreath [33 cm] diameter of [cm]

16 sc and 16 rows = 4 ins [10 cm].

BELL 8

Ch 2 with B.

1st rnd: (RS). 6 sc in the second ch from the hook. In the first sc, join with ss.

Ch 1 in the second rnd. 1 sc in each sc all the way around to the first sc, join with ss.

Third round: Ch 1. 1 sc in each of the first two sc

2 sc in the next sc 1 sc in each of the next 2 rows

sc. 2 sc in the next sc Join ss in first sc. 8 sc.

Fourth round: Ch 1. 1 sc in the same st as the last ss. (2 sc in the next sc, 1 sc in the following sc) 3times. 2 sc in the next sc Join forces with ss in the first sc 12 sc.

Fifth to seventh rnds: Ch 1. 1 sc in the same st as in the previous ss 1 sc in each sc all the way around. Join with a ss in the first sc Fasten off at end of the

7th rnd.

Finishing: Cut the wire to the appropriate length as well as a glue bead at one end Insert

Insert the other end of the wire into the Bell and secure it with glue in the position depicted

CHAPTER 5

Holiday Leaf 9

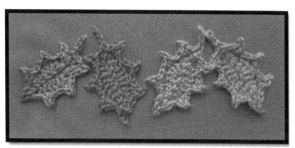

ch 11 with A

1st rnd: (RS). 1 sc in the 2nd ch from the hook. 1 sc in the next ch (1 hdc.

 Ch 2. 1

hdc) in the following chapter 1 hdc each in the next two chapters (1 dc. Ch 2. 1 dc) all in the next row

ch. 1 dc in the following ch 1 hdc each in the next two chapters 1 sc, 3 ch, 1 sc) all in last ch.Continue working on the other side of the ch. 1 hdc in each of the next two ch 1 dc in the following ch (1 dc, 2 ch, 1 dc) all in the following chapter 1 hdc in each of the next two chains (1 hdc. Ch 2. 1 hdc) in the next ch 1 sc in the following chapter 1 sc in the last ch Ch 2. Join forces with ss to the first sc Close the loop.

Assembly

Glue Leaves, using the photo as a guide.

Clusters of bells and tiny bows

illustrated. Wreath with glue clusters. G\lue a large bow to the top of the wreath as shown. illustrated. Glue pinecones to the

As shown, make a wreath.

WREATH PIN FOR CHRISTMAS 10

Crochet a small Christmas wreath for a pin or hanging ornament. The crochet Christmas wreath sparkles with light-reflecting mixing filaments.

Materials:

•Crochet cotton size 10: a little bit of green (A) •Crochet cotton size 20: small amounts of red (B) and yellow (C)

•Green #008 (BFA) and red 003HL Kreinik Blending Filaments (50 m per spool): 1 spool each (BFB)

•Steel crochet hook size 7 or size required to reach gauge

•Size 9 steel crochet hook •12-inch length 1/4-inch wide Christmas ribbon •1-inch long pin back •Tapestry needle •Embroidery needle •Sewing needle and green sewing thread

Rnds 1 and 2 of the wreath = 1-3/8 inch in diameter with a bigger hook.

To save time, check the gauge.

Instructions:

Pattern Unless otherwise specified, join rounds with a sl st.

Stitch Pattern: Insert hook into the next st, yo, draw up an lp, [yo, draw through 1 lp on hook] Yo, draw through rem 2 lps on hook 4 times, moving lp to RS of work.

Rnd 1

\Rnd 1 Ch 24, join to form a ring, ch 1, lp st in same st as joining, sc in next st, [lp st in next st, sc in next st] rep around, join in first lp st (24 sts)

Rnd 2: Ch 1; sc in same st as joining, *lp st in next st, [sc, lp st] in next st**, sc in next st, rep from * around, finishing last rep at **, join in first sc.

(32 sts)

Rnd 3: Ch 1, lp st in same st as joining, *sc in next st, lp st in next st, [sc, lp st] in next st, sc in next st, lp st in next st, sc in next st, [lp st, sc] in next st**, lp st in (40 sts)

Rnd 4: Ch 1, sc in same st as joining, *lp st in next st, sc in next st, lp st in next st, sc in next st, [sc, lp st] in next st**, sc in next st, rep from * around, ending last rep at **, join in beg sc. (48 sts)

Rnd 5: Ch 1, lp st in same st as connecting, *sc in next st, lp st in next st, sc in next st, lp st in next st, sc in next st, lp st in next st, sc in next st, lp st in next st,

POINSETTIA (make 4): ch 1 (central ch), [ch 5, sl st in center ch] 6 times, fasten off, leaving length for finishing.

Finishing

Make a bow out of Christmas ribbon and tack it to the bottom of the wreath on the WS with a sewing needle and green thread.

Tack 4 poinsettias evenly placed around center of wreath with lengths remaining for completing and tapestry needle.

Make a french knot in the middle of each poinsettia using an embroidery needle and C. With a sewing needle and green sewing thread, attach the pin back to the top back of the wreath. Spray starch the front of the wreath.

Christmas Wreath Crochet

Lily Sugar'n Cream's

For this free crochet patterned Christmas wreath, crochet festive miniature stockings, wrapped presents, and Santas. Crocheting each motif is quick, making this a delightful Christmas activity.

•Yarn: Lily Sugar'n Cream Cotton 4 plies Solids Sparkles/2.5 oz [70.9 g] 2 oz [56.7 g]

1 Sugar'n Cream (Emerald) ball to wrap Wreath \s(optional)

A color - (Red) 1 color B ball - (Baby Pink) 1 color C ball - (White) 1 D-colored ball (Mistletoe Sparkle) 1 \sball

A small amount of blue yarn is used.

•Crochet hook: 4 mm (US G or 6) crochet hook or size required for gauge

•Glue gun and glue sticks •2 yards [1.8 meters] of 5/8 inch [15 mm] wide green ribbon

•3 yards [2.75 meters] of white ribbon, 1/4 inch [10 mm] wide •20 little dried pine cones

- ☐ Styrofoam 12 in [30.5 cm] diameter wreath

Please keep in mind that 1 ball of A, B, and C makes 15 Santas. 7 Stockings are made from 1 ball of A and 1 ball of C. 1 Sparkle ball

5 Gift Boxes are created.

16 stitches and 16 rows = 4 ins [10 cm]

CHAPTER 6

Santa 11

Face: With B, ch 6 and sl st together to form a ring.

First round: Ch 3, 7 dc in ring. Break B and join C in the final dc. 8 dc in the same ring with C. In the first dc, sl st.

Ch 3 and sl st in top of first B st.

Sl st in top of next st, ch 3.

* For all B sts, rep from * to *.

Sl st into the next C st. ** Rep from ** to ** to complete the ring. Close the loop.

Hat: ch 9 with A.

1st row: 1 sc in the second ch from the hook. 1 sc in each sc to the end of the ch. 8 sc 2nd row: Ch 1, skip first sc. 1 sc in each sc till row is finished. Turn.

Rep the second row until just one stitch remains.

Close the loop.

Join C with a sl st to the point of the hat for the pompom. Ch 4 and sl st together to form a ring.

First round: Ch 1, 12 sc in ring.

Break yarn leaving a 6-inch (15-cm) tail.

Draw a needle through the top of each stitch in the ring.

Draw up tightly and secure.

FINISHING: Sew Hat on Face as shown. Using blue yarn, embroider two eyeballs.

STOCKING 12

Cuff: ch 13 with C.

1st row: (RS). 1 sc in the 2nd ch from the hook 1 sc in each ch till the end of the ch 12 \ssc. Turn with the first ch.

2nd row: 1 sc in each sc until row is finished. Turn with the first ch.

Rep the second row once again, joining A at the end of the last row.

Leg: 1 sc in each sc till the end of the row with A. Turn with the first ch.

Rep final row until work measures 3 ins [7.5 cm] from beginning, ending with RS facing and omitting turning ch at end of last row. Close the loop.

Heel: With the RS of the work facing you, miss the first 9 sc. Sl st in the next sc to join C.

1 sc in the first ch. 1 sc in each of the last two sc Turn the opposite leg around. 1 sc

in each of the first 3 sc Turn. Next row: 1 sc in each of the first 4 sc. Turn. Next row: 1 sc in each of the first 2 sc. Turn. Next row: 1 sc in each of the next 2 sc. 1 sc in the next sc in the lengthy row below 3 sts.

Turn. Next row: 1 sc in each of the next 3 sc. 1 sc in the next sc in the lengthy row below 4 sts.

Turn with the first ch.

Continue as in the previous two rows until 6 sts of Heel have been knitted, omitting the turning ch at the end of the final row. Fasten \soff.

Miss the first three sc of Heel with the RS of the work facing. Sl st in the next sc to join A. 1 sc in the first ch. 1 sc in each of the next 2 sc of the heel Leg's next sc is missed. 1 sc in each of the next four sc

Leg's next sc is missed. 1 sc in each of the next 3 sc of the heel Turn with the first ch. 10 sts.

Row 2: 1 sc in each sc till the end of the row. Turn with the first ch.

Row 2: 1 sc in each sc to the end of the row, changing to C in the last sc. Toe: Ch 1, turn. Next 2 rows: 1 sc in each sc till the end of the row with C Turn. Next row: (Draw a loop in each of the next two rows. 5 times, draw a loop across all loops on hook (Sc2tog formed). Close the loop.

Finishing: Sew the cuff and back seams of the leg. Sew the toe and foot seams. Sew the heel's corners closed. Lightly stuff.

BOX OF GIFT 13

Box's main component: ch 8 with D

1st row: 1 sc in the second ch from the hook. 1 sc in each ch till the end of the ch Turn and make 7 sc. **2nd to 6th rows: 1 sc in each sc to the end of the row Turn. 7th row: Ch 1, 1 sc in back loop only of each sc till row is finished. 8th to 10th rows: Turn. 1 sc in each sc to the end of the row **11th row: repeat 7th row. Rep once from ** to **. Close the loop.

Sides of the box: (make 2)

1st row: 1 sc in the 2nd ch from hook. 1 sc in each ch till the end of the row 6 sc, turn

Rows 2–4: Ch 1, 1 sc in each sc to end of row. Turn. Close the loop.

Finishing: Sew the first row of the Main Piece to the last row to make a box with open sides. Sew one Box Side in place. Box of Stuff Sew the remaining Box Side in place. Wrap a length of ribbon around the box, tie a bow, and stitch it shut.

Assembly

Wrap yarn around the Styrofoam Wreath to completely cover it if desired. Glue Santas, Stockings, and Gift Boxes to Wreath as shown, using the photo as a guide. Glue pine cones and a ribbon bow on top.

Crochet a lovely white wreath with red beads and ribbon for a Christmas ornament. Make many crochet wreaths to decorate your Christmas tree or to give as gifts this season. Ashton11 has provided us with this pattern.

•Knitting worsted yarn (or 100% cotton worsted, or satiny yarn of any kind) •Crochet Hook, size 6MM (USJ 10) •Assorted beads

•A pipecleaner with a white chenille stem •A hot glue gun and a glue stick, or white glue

1. Cut a chenille stem into an oval of any size. Make a huge oval out of the full chenille stem, or link two together to make a large window hanging.

2. Tie the yarn to the chenille stem in whatever way you like. You may either knot it or slip stitch it on.

3. Use the following sequence to cover the entire shape, pulling the stitches together to fit as many as needed:

Single crochet three times around the stem. Treat the stem as though it were a previous row of stitches. Make 3 single crochet chains. Repeat all the way around the shape. To join, use a slip stitch.

4. Form a hanger by tying red velvet ribbon into a loop. Spot glue hot glue sparingly onto the top of the oval.

5. Build a bow with as many loops as you want, or make numerous bows and hot glue them together sparingly.

6. Sew or use tiny spots of hot glue (applied directly to the bead, not the yarn) to adhere.

Voila! A stunning Christmas ornament for the tree, a window, a present, or a Christmas card!

5 Gift Boxes are created.

16 stitches and 16 rows = 4 ins [10 cm]

Made in United States
Orlando, FL
05 December 2024

55000981R10033